Building Character
Having Empathy

by Penelope S. Nelson

Bullfrog Books

Ideas for Parents and Teachers

Bullfrog Books let children practice reading informational text at the earliest reading levels. Repetition, familiar words, and photo labels support early readers.

Before Reading

- Discuss the cover photo. What does it tell them?

- Look at the picture glossary together. Read and discuss the words.

Read the Book

- "Walk" through the book and look at the photos. Let the child ask questions. Point out the photo labels.

- Read the book to the child, or have him or her read independently.

After Reading

- Prompt the child to think more. Ask: Did you know what empathy was before reading this book? How do you show empathy?

Bullfrog Books are published by Jump!
5357 Penn Avenue South
Minneapolis, MN 55419
www.jumplibrary.com

Library of Congress Cataloging-in-Publication Data

Names: Nelson, Penelope, 1994– author.
Title: Having empathy / by Penelope S. Nelson.
Description: Minneapolis, MN: Jump!, Inc., 2020.
Series: Building character | Includes index.
Audience: Age 5–8. | Audience: K to Grade 3.
Identifiers: LCCN 2018046168 (print)
LCCN 2018047620 (ebook)
ISBN 9781641287197 (ebook)
ISBN 9781641287173 (hardcover)
ISBN 9781641287180 (pbk.)
Subjects: LCSH: Empathy—Juvenile literature.
Classification: LCC BF575.E55 (ebook) | LCC BF575.E55 N45 2020 (print) | DDC 152.4/1—dc23
LC record available at https://lccn.loc.gov/2018046168

Editor: Jenna Trnka
Designer: Michelle Sonnek

Photo Credits: KK Tan/Shutterstock, cover; MilamPhotos/iStock, 1; all_about_people/Shutterstock, 3; wavebreakmedia/Shutterstock, 4, 6–7, 10–11, 18; Yobro10/iStock, 5, 23bl; Biserka Stojanovic/Shutterstock, 8–9; paulaphoto/Shutterstock, 12; Starik_73/Shutterstock, 13; LightField Studios/Shutterstock, 14–15; fstop123/iStock, 16–17, 23br; Apollofoto/Shutterstock, 19; Image Source/iStock, 20–21, 23tl; Tungphoto/Shutterstock, 22l; FabrikaSimf/Shutterstock, 22r; KUNG MIN JU/Shutterstock, 23tr; Dave Pot/Shutterstock, 24.

Printed in the United States of America at Corporate Graphics in North Mankato, Minnesota.

Table of Contents

Understanding Others 4

Many Kinds of Feelings 22

Picture Glossary 23

Index 24

To Learn More 24

Understanding Others

What is empathy?

It means being sensitive.
To what? How other people feel.
We try to understand them.

Roy goes to a new school.

He feels lonely.

Sam sits with him.

Nice!

Mia cries.
She misses her mom.

Joe hugs Mia.
He misses his mom
sometimes, too.

Our friend is mad.

We think of when we were mad.

It felt bad.

We understand our friend.

Tia's dog is lost.

Pat doesn't have a pet.
But he listens to Tia's feelings.
He helps her. They find it!

Joy falls.
Ouch!
Ned helps.

Gia and her sister fight.

They talk.

They both listen.

To what?

Each other's feelings.

May got a good grade.
She is happy.

grade

Tim is happy for her!

19

How do you show empathy?

Many Kinds of Feelings

There are many kinds of feelings. Write a list of all of the feelings you know. What made you feel them? What feelings do people around you have? Ask siblings, friends, or caregivers how they feel. If you don't understand, ask them why they feel those emotions. Does it help you understand? You are showing empathy!

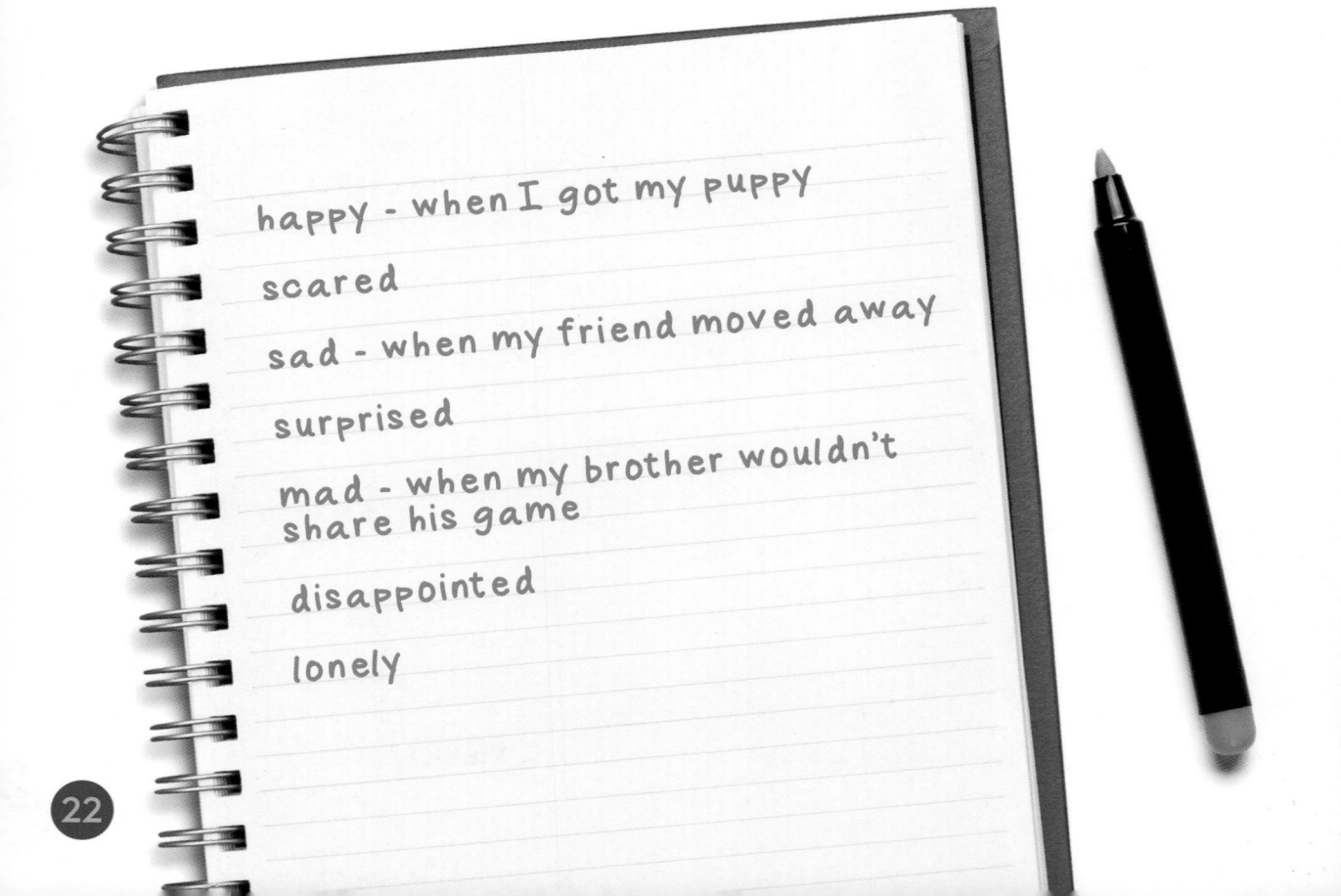

happy - when I got my puppy

scared

sad - when my friend moved away

surprised

mad - when my brother wouldn't share his game

disappointed

lonely

Picture Glossary

empathy
The ability to understand, be sensitive to, and care about the feelings of others.

lonely
Missing the company of other people.

sensitive
Aware of another's feelings, attitudes, or situation.

understand
To have sympathy for someone or grasp the meaning of how they feel.

To Learn More

Finding more information is as easy as 1, 2, 3.

① Go to www.factsurfer.com
② Enter "havingempathy" into the search box.
③ Click the "Surf" button to see a list of websites.

Index

cries 8
empathy 4, 20
feelings 13, 17
happy 18, 19
helps 13, 14
hugs 8
listens 13, 17
lonely 7
mad 11
sensitive 5
talk 17
understand 5, 11